Yogiji Maharaj's TALES OF WISDOM

Book 2

Know the True You

Swaminarayan Aksharpith
Ahmedabad

Yogiji Maharaj's Tales of Wisdom: Book 2

Know the True You

Inspirer: HH Mahant Swami Maharaj

Authors: Ashmi Patel, Sejal Maisuria & Dhwani Tank
Editor: Komal Parikh
Illustrator: Ishani Patel
Colorist: Mugdha Rege
Special Thanks: Amita Rao, Bindi Patel, Deepa Gohill, Kreena Amin, Ria Soni, Amisha Bhavsar, Shivang Danak & Tejas Jivrajani
Layout: Radheshyam Patel
Series Editor: Sadhu Mangalnidhidas

Presented by:
BAPS North America Publications Team
and
Children's Activities Central Office
BAPS Swaminarayan Sanstha
Shahibaug, Ahmedabad-380 004, Gujarat, India

1st Edition: May 2023
Copies: 7,000
ISBN: 978-1-947461-21-5

Published & Printed by
Swaminarayan Aksharpith

Shahibaug Road, Ahmedabad, India
Website: www.baps.org | http://kids.baps.org

Dear Parents,

Know the True You is about Sheru, an orphan lion cub, found by a shepherd and raised with a herd of sheep. Sheru grows up thinking he is a sheep like the others, but he is able to discover his true identity with the guidance of the majestic lion, Keshav. Through Sheru's journey, we hope to help our little ones realize their true spiritual identity as the *atma* (soul), thus providing them a solid foundation for the development of spiritual virtues.

This story is inspired by the *101 Tales of Wisdom*, a collection of parables told by Yogiji Maharaj, the fourth spiritual successor of Bhagwan Swaminarayan. While Yogiji Maharaj referred to the lion cub as Lindiyo, and here he is named Sheru, the rest of the story is the same. Yogiji Maharaj's Tales of Wisdom inspire the cultivation of virtues such as unity, hard work, humility, spirituality, and altruism.

This children's book series by Swaminarayan Aksharpith provides parents and children a platform to explore these universal truths. We believe that the development of such values within oneself and one's family encourages peace and understanding within the home and, by extension, within one's community and society at large.

From,
The Authors

"The essence of all spiritual wisdom is to know yourself as the atma."

- Mahant Swami Maharaj

One day, a lost lion cub sat scared and alone, longing to be reunited with his family.

A shepherd stumbled upon the tiny, frightened cub and decided to bring him home. "I am going to name you Sheru! Let me leave you with the other animals so you can make friends."

"Hi, Sheru! My name is Bholu, and this is Bholi! Let's go play together!"

Soon, Bholu, Bholi, and Sheru became the best of friends.

As they played, they came upon a steep cliff.
Bholu and Bholi bleated cheerfully into
the canyon below, delighted to hear their echo back.

"Sheru, bleat with us too," Bholu said. Sheru opened his mouth and out came a booming, "BAAAAAARRRRRRR!"

Bholu and Bholi shook their heads.
"That is not a bleat, Sheru.
Let us show you how it is done."

Sheru practiced and practiced, until finally, "I think I am getting the hang of it!" he shouted with glee.

Little did the three friends know that they had been seen from a distance by none other than the mighty lion, Keshav.

14

"Who is that lion cub, and why is he bleating with those sheep?" Keshav wondered. "I must get a closer look."

In the next instant,
the trio ran for their lives.
But in just a few leaps,
Keshav caught Sheru by the tail.
"Not so fast, little cub. Who are you?"
Keshav asked.

"I-I-I am... Sheru, the sheep.
P-Please, let me go!"

18

"My dear confused lion cub,
you are not a sheep!
Come with me.
I will show you
who you really are," Keshav said.

19

Sheru's mind was spinning.
"Why did he call me a lion cub?
Am I a lion cub?
Are my friends lion cubs too?"

"Sheru, take a look at yourself in the water.
Now take a look at me.
What do you see?"

"We both have golden hair!"
Sheru said with surprise.

Keshav responded,
"That's called a mane!"

22

Sheru continued,
"We both have these large hooves."

"Those are called paws.
My friend, you are a lion!" explained Keshav.

"I am a lion? Is this why I did not sound like my friends when I first tried to bleat?" Sheru asked.

Keshav nodded. "Exactly! Lions do not bleat; we roar.
Let me teach you how.

First, stand proud
and unafraid.
Then, with courage
and conviction,
you must roar like this....

ROAAAAARRRRRRR!!!"

Sheru
mustered all
his strength and
let out a loud...

"ROOaaaa-baaaa...."

Keshav laughed.
"In your heart,
some part of you still thinks
you are a sheep.

Only when you fully know
the true you will you be able
to find your roar."

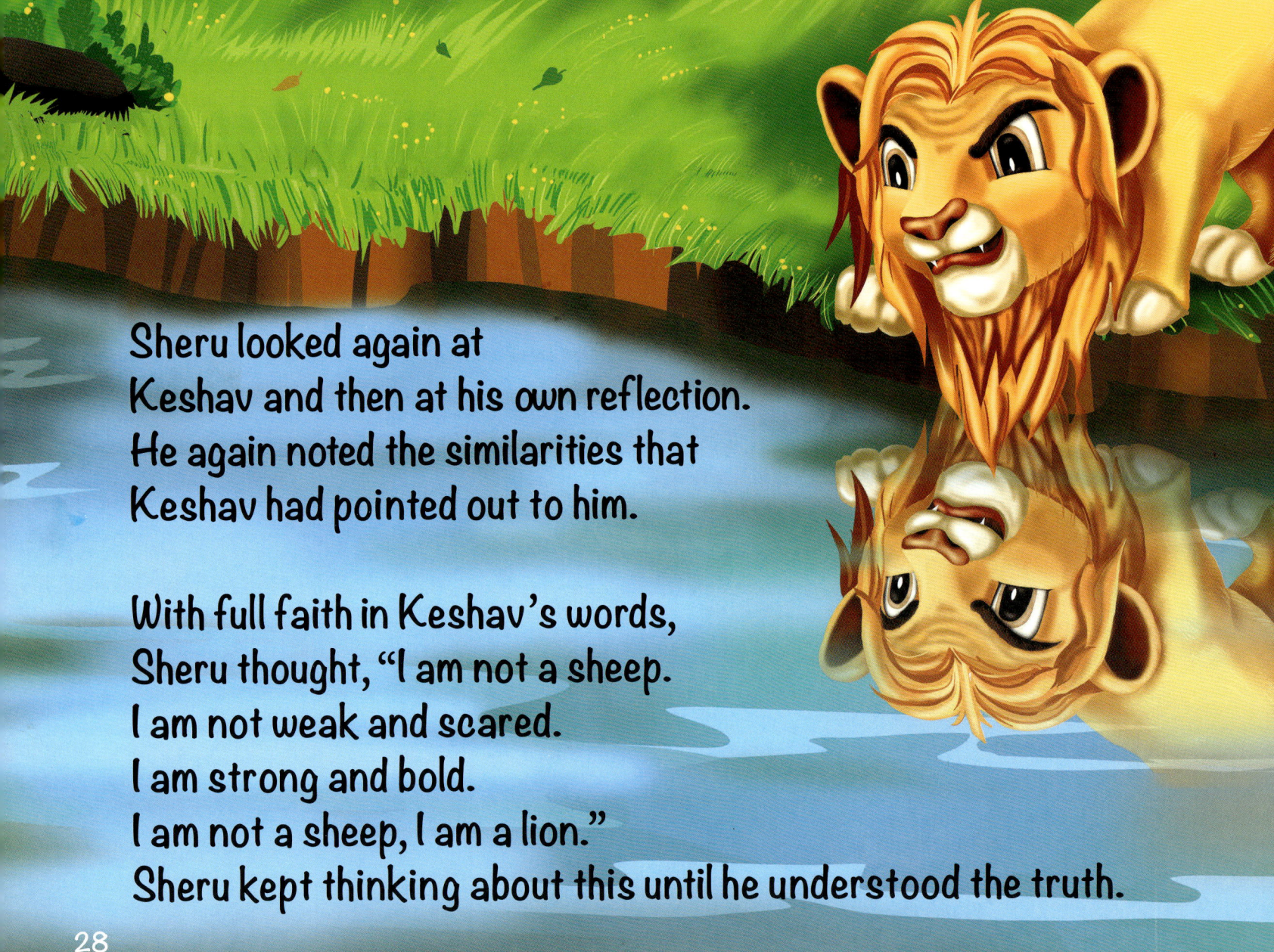

Sheru looked again at
Keshav and then at his own reflection.
He again noted the similarities that
Keshav had pointed out to him.

With full faith in Keshav's words,
Sheru thought, "I am not a sheep.
I am not weak and scared.
I am strong and bold.
I am not a sheep, I am a lion."
Sheru kept thinking about this until he understood the truth.

With a new, determined spirit,
Sheru stood tall and let out
a huge, loud....

"ROOAARRR!"

"I knew you could do it," Keshav exclaimed proudly. "How do you feel?"

"I finally feel like myself. All this time, I was surrounded by sheep. So, I thought I was one. But now I'm a lion, just like you!"

"Sheru, you were always a lion. You just didn't realize it."

With an understanding of his true self, Sheru walked off to join Keshav and his pride.

"...and so children, the story of Sheru shows us that
we, too, can learn our true identity
as the *atma* from a true guru.
Let us take a closer look at Sheru's journey."

Family Discussion Corner

As a result of the company that he kept, Sheru believed that he was a sheep.

Similarly, *kusang*, or bad company, convinces us that we are this physical body and prevents us from "knowing the true you."

What represents the 'sheep' in our lives?

Sheru learned about his identity as a lion with the guidance of Keshav. Keshav represents the guru, a spiritual teacher who leads us from untruth to truth.

We also need to learn from a true guru like Mahant Swami Maharaj to understand the truth about who we are.

How did Keshav help Sheru understand who he is?

When Sheru looked at himself in the lake, he was thinking about who he was. He was a lion and not a sheep!

Likewise, we need to reflect that we are the *atma* and not the body. The *atma* is the immortal core of each living being. Our *atma* is our true, eternal self, filled with pure joy!

What are some actions or thoughts that can help us remember that we are the *atma*?

By directly following Keshav's instructions and having faith in his words, Sheru learned to transform his bleat into a roar.

Just as Sheru learned from Keshav how to be a fearless lion, what things can we learn from our guru to help us behave as the *atma*?

Sheru's story teaches us
that by having faith in the guru's words and
following the guru's guidance,
you will understand your true self
to be greater than this physical body.
You will know the true you to be the *atma*.

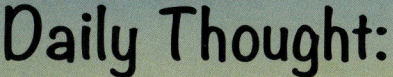

Daily Thought:

"I am not the body. I am the *atma*. I am Akshar.
I am happy, smart, eternal, and strong.
I am a lion; I am not a sheep. I am the *atma*; I am not this body.

Believing I am the *atma*
and behaving
as the *atma* will bring me
joy and please my guru."

39

Swaminarayan Aksharpith has publications for children of all ages.
You can find them at your local BAPS Mandir Bookstore or find online at baps.store.

Adventures of Ghanshyam

Book 1
The Birth of Ghanshyam

Book 2
Ghanshyam Gets His Name

Book 3
The Coin, the Scripture, and the Sword

Book 4
Ghanshyam Gets His Ears Pierced

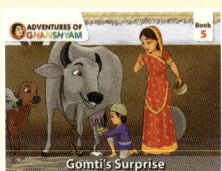
Book 5
Gomti's Surprise

Book 6
Ghanshyam Gets His First Haircut

Book 7
Ghanshyam Defeats Kalidatta

Book 8
The Fisherman's Choice

Book 9
Ghanshyam Teaches Ramdatta Respect

Book 10
Ghanshyam Looks West

- 108 Prasang Mala: Inspiring Satsang Stories
- Bal Satsang Exam Book Series: Satsang Vihar Part 1
- Bal Satsang Exam Book Series: Satsang Vihar Part 2
- Bal Satsang Exam Book Series: Satsang Vihar Part 3
- Sucharitam Part 1 to 5: Value Stories for Children
- Swamishri - Our Best Friend
- Story Time Part 1 & 2
- Let's Follow Shanti's Way
- The Tales of the Bal Nagari
- PSM Nagar Activity Book
- Buzo And The Dangers of The Jungle
- Shikshapatri: Children's Illustrated Version
- Kidi and Mr. Hathi
- Study Techniques - Effective Study Techniques for School Students

- Swaminarayan Bal Prakash 'Bimonthly Magazine'
- Good Habits Bad Habits
- Yogi And The Magical Sage
- Pictorial: Bhagwan Swaminarayan
- Pictorial: Aksharbrahman Gunatitanand Swami

Shri Swaminarayan Charitra

View Full Animated Movies in Hindi and English Available Online

Part 1
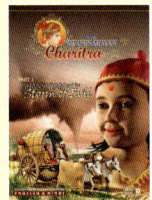
Ghanshyam and the Storm of Evil

Part 2

Ghanshyam and the Miracles of Life

Part 3

Ghanshyam and the Aura of Ayodhya

Part 4
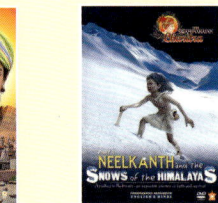
Neelkanth and the Snows of the Himalayas

Part 5

Neelkanth and the Swans of Mansarovar

SCAN QR CODE:

OR VISIT US AT:
https://www.baps.org